Who's Who
in a
Neighborhood

Jake Miller

The Rosen Publishing Group's
PowerKids Press™
New York

Published in 2005 by The Rosen Publishing Group, Inc.
29 East 21st Street, New York, NY 10010

First Edition

Editor: Joanne Randolph
Book Design: Maria E. Melendez
Layout Design: Emily Muschinske

Photo Credits: Cover, p. 1 © Royalty-Free/CORBIS; p. 5 © Jason Hawkes/CORBIS; p. 7 © Bill Ross/CORBIS; p. 9 © Ariel Skelley/CORBIS; p. 11 © Tom Stewart/CORBIS; p. 13 © Ed Bock/CORBIS; p. 15 Denis Scott/CORBIS; p. 17 © STEVEN E. FRISCHLING/CORBIS SYGMA; p. 19 © Joseph Sohm; ChromoSohm Inc./CORBIS; p. 21 © Paul Barton/CORBIS.

Library of Congress Cataloging-in-Publication Data

Miller, Jake, 1969–
Who's who in a neighborhood / Jake Miller.
    v. cm. — (Communities at work)
Includes bibliographical references and index.
Contents: Together in the neighborhood — Living and working in town — Growing up in the neighborhood — At home on the block — Working in the neighborhood — The community center — Cleaning up the streets — Everyone helps out — Having fun with the neighbors — Life in a neighborhood.
ISBN 1-4042-2785-7 (library bind.) – ISBN1-4042-5024-7 (pbk.)
1. Neighborhood—Juvenile literature. 2. Community life—Juvenile literature. 3. Cities and towns—Juvenile literature. [1. Neighborhood. 2. Community life. 3. Cities and towns.] I. Title. II. Series.

HM761.M55 2005
307.3'362—dc22

2003025685

Manufactured in the United States of America

Contents

Together in the Neighborhood

A **community** is a group of people who live and work together. It is also the place in which these people live.

Neighborhoods are a kind of community. They are made up of the people who live, work, and play in a small part of a city or a town.

All the houses on one street in a town can make up a neighborhood. The people on the street help each other. A person may take care of a neighbor's pet or share gardening tips.

Many Neighborhoods

There are different kinds of neighborhoods. A single **apartment** building might be a neighborhood in a city. Towns have neighborhoods, too. The neighborhood might be a single street. It might be a few streets in one area of the town. The people in the neighborhood help each other with the things that they need.

In a city neighborhood, the homes are close together. Some buildings are home to just one family. Other buildings are home to hundreds of families.

Growing Up in the Neighborhood

A lot of children live in a neighborhood community. These children may play together. They may share the same bus stop. Older children may babysit the younger children in a neighborhood. Children help bring neighborhood communities together.

Some neighborhood communities have a playground. The playground is a place where children in the neighborhood can meet to play.

Help in the Neighborhood

People in the neighborhood help each other. One man likes to mow the lawn. When his neighbor is sick, he mows her lawn for her. She babysits for his children when he and his wife want to go out. Everyone in the neighborhood has ways that they can help someone else.

The teens are trying to make money for the nearby animal shelter. These teenagers rake leaves from a neighbor's yard. The neighbor pays them for their work.

Working at the Community Center

The community center is a place where people from the neighborhood can spend time together. The people who work at the center are an important part of the community. Some people who work at the center are paid for their work. Other people give their time for free. They want to help other people in the community.

A community center worker helps a child with her art project. The community center is a place to learn, and a place to have fun! ▷

Working in the Neighborhood

Not everyone in the community lives in the neighborhood. Some people live in other places but come to the neighborhood every day to work. The plumber comes to fix people's sinks, tubs, and pipes. The neighbors cannot do everything by themselves. They need help from people from other places, too.

The mail carrier delivers letters and packages to all the neighbors. He may not live in the neighborhood but he is an important part of the community.

Cleaning Up the Streets

It takes a lot of different people to keep the streets of the neighborhood clean. In many neighborhoods, the town pays a company to pick up the **garbage**. The town also sends street sweepers and **snowplows** to keep neighborhood roads clean.

Snowplows clear away the snow so that people in the neighborhood can drive safely.

Working Together

Some projects are too big for one person. Sometimes everyone has to work together. Some communities have a neighborhood clean-up day each year. The local hardware store may **donate** garbage bags and work gloves. Neighbors work in teams. Some teams pick up **litter**. Some clean out empty lots. Together they make the neighborhood a better place.

People work together to make their neighborhood a nice place to live. These people are clearing away weeds to plant a garden.

Having Fun with the Neighbors

Being part of a community is not all hard work. Neighbors like to have fun together, too. In the summer, a neighborhood might have a block party. Some people cook food on the grill. Others bring salads and desserts. They all share their food and eat together.

Neighbors enjoy a summer day together. An important part of being in a community is spending time with your neighbors.

Life in a Neighborhood

A neighborhood is a place where people feel like they belong. They know that their neighbors will help them when they have a problem. They know that the men and women who work in the neighborhood will help them to get what they need. They are a community, and they can count on each other!

Glossary

apartment (uh-PART-ment) Describing a building in which many people live.

community (kuh-MYOO-nih-tee) A place where people live and work together, or the people who make up such a place.

donate (DOH-nayt) To give to a person or group without charging money to help that person or group do something good.

garbage (GAR-bij) Things that are thrown away.

litter (LIH-ter) Trash that is thrown on the ground instead of being placed in a bag or a trash can.

neighborhoods (NAY-ber-hudz) Places where people live together.

snowplows (SNOH-plowz) Machines used to clear away snow.

Index

Web Sites

Due to the changing nature of Internet links, PowerKids Press has developed an online list of Web sites related to the subject of this book. This site is updated regularly. Please use this link to access the list: www.powerkidslinks.com/caw/whoneigh/